SPARKS OF
PHOENIX

ALSO BY NAJWA ZEBIAN

Mind Platter
The Nectar of Pain

SPARKS OF PHOENIX

NAJWA ZEBIAN

Andrews McMeel
PUBLISHING®

CONTENTS

PROLOGUE

To heal from your pain
now,
you need to go all the way back
to chapter one.
To page one.
To the beginning
of how it all began.

For every ending,
there is a
once upon a time.
For every broken soul,
there is a
once upon a happy soul.
For every phoenix soaring,
there is a phoenix
burning,
turning to ashes,
rising,
then soaring.

Let me hand you the matches
to ignite the glory
within your soul.
Let me be the one
who burns to ashes
as you spark in your darkest of nights.
As you rise.
As you soar.

I

THE BURNING

You lit my soul
on fire
and told me
to watch it burn.

He asks me:
"What do you want from me?"
I stare at him in silence
with tears fighting to stay
buried inside my eyes,
with thoughts swirling in my mind
like a hurricane.
"What do you want from me?" he asks
over and over.

I am confused because
I know and
I don't know.

You were the one
who knocked on my door.
You were the one
who wouldn't allow me to close my door.

He told me
that he loved how
I made him feel.
Back then,
I put my self-worth
in his hands
and told him
"Be the master."

He attached strings to my self-worth
and played with me
like a marionette.

I used to look at those in pain
and think
they are choosing to be in pain
until pain chose me
and I understood the taste
of feeling pain
that you cannot control.

I see myself crumbling
and my wings
becoming weaker and weaker,
but there is nothing I can do.
It feels like
there is poison running through
my veins
and I am letting go
one breath at a time.

I go back and forth
between being angry with you
and falling back into the moments
I fell in love with you.

One moment,
I want to scream at you,
the next moment,
I want to tell you
I love you.

My heart crumbles
into my aching soul
because I know that
I will never get the answer,
but all I want to ask you is:
Why did you ask me to love you
when you had no intention
of loving me?

You don't know
how dangerous it is
for me to see you.

I start living time
in reverse.
My anger with you
starts to fade.
My hatred for what you did
begins to escape.
And I arrive right at the moments
when I fell in love with you.

Run away
because that is what you do best.
You break a heart then
run away.
You shatter a soul then
run away.
You say that you no longer care,
and you think that makes you strong.
Don't you know that
the greatest act of courage is to love?
What a fool you are for running away.

My soul has been burning
for a while now.
Pain has become
my new normal.

I cannot differentiate between
excruciating pain
and pain that feels
less painful.
It's all the same.

After all this time,
I wonder how you're doing.
My bones tell me
to be angry with you
for walking away when you
promised not to.
But my heart pretends
to understand you
and gives excuses for you.
Do you miss me?
Or did I become like
one of the streets in
one of the cities that
you once visited:
a distant memory
that you don't remember unless
you see a picture of me
or read a poem that you once
allowed your heart to write
to me
or
about me?

My heart hurts,
and I am not sure
which part of it
is aching the most.

I do not want anyone to tell me
to stop feeling the pain.
I do not want anyone to tell me
to let things go.

I do not want anyone to tell me
I am overthinking this.
I just want someone to
love me through this.

I saw you from a distance
and felt sad.
I knew you wouldn't come to me
like you used to.
But you did come to me
like you used to
and lay by my side
like you used to.
You ran your fingers
across my face
and the creases of my hands
like you used to.
You were gentle with me
and took a few moments
to look deeply into my eyes
like you used to.
My soul flooded with happiness,
but soon I woke up
from my dream
because you no longer love me
like you used to.

If your heart hurts a little after letting go of someone or something, that's okay. It just means that your feelings were genuine. No one likes endings. And no one likes pain. But sometimes we have to put things that were once good to an end after they turn toxic to our well-being. Not every new beginning is meant to last forever. And not every person who walks into your life is meant to stay.

You seek pain as if
it's going to save you.
You dip into sadness
as if it's going to bring you joy.
You expect that loving
the night will make
your days better,
and that loving the rain
will make the sun shine brighter.
You expect that diving
into the ocean
will get you to the shore of sanity
faster.

Perhaps we live life in opposites.
To feel one thing,
we seek the other.
To become a masterpiece,
we seek to be undone,
to create a self
so delicately stitched together,
it cannot be compared to another.

I am burning
to ashes,
hoping to rise one day.

Every time he asked me
"Who do you think you are?"
the ashes that I was
burning into
would answer:
"I am no one."

I bled,
almost to death.
Almost.

You make the mistake
then blame me for it.
You say I pushed you
to be angry.
And every time I try to apologize,
you don't accept my apology.

That's called gaslighting.

If they take advantage of your vulnerability, they should be ashamed, not you. Vulnerability takes courage. Taking advantage takes cowardice. And though the world may be filled with people ready to take advantage of your purity, don't let them taint your heart. The world might bring you down for being your kind self, but don't let that change you. The world might push you to believe that there is no place for good people, but don't let that stop you from believing in goodness. And if you struggle with the darkness out there, the world might convince you that you're too sensitive. But don't let that stop you from feeling. If feeling the pain of unfairness makes you sensitive, then may we all be sensitive. What I'm trying to say is, if you make the choice to be a good person regardless of how the world treats you in return, be proud of that. It makes you a hero. A gem. A true human.

Through all of the pain
that your heart is drowning in,
your heart is still beating.
It is resilient, and
so are you.
Learn from that.

I run from
place to place,
wanting to belong,
wanting to find a home.
When will I learn that
my home is within me
and it comes with me
everywhere I go?

You think that time will change them. It won't. You think
that they'll realize their mistakes with time and run to you for
forgiveness. They won't. They will not. They. Will. Not. Let it sink
in. Narcissists always believe that they are right. Once you become
nothing to them, you are absolutely nothing. And after you expose
their true colors, they start seeing you as the devil and run the
other direction when you should be the one running away, further
making you feel like you're not worthy of their presence. It will
bother you that they can be so heartless when they are the ones at
fault. But remember: At least you have a heart. At least you can
feel. Be grateful for that.

I saw you,
and you looked like the weight
of the world was on your shoulders.
I felt guilty and
wanted to ask you
how you were doing.
But my heart reminded me:
You're the one who chose to leave.
You're the one who chose to hurt me.
You're the one who chose the end.
So I will let you deal with this pain
on your own.
If you deserved my care,
you would have loved me
when you had the chance.
So I put my heart together and
I walked away,
not because I didn't care
but because the heart that you broke
couldn't handle being broken again.

What is worse
than destroying someone
is making them believe
it was their fault.

That's what you did to me.

They mutilate your soul
by silencing
your voice.
So anytime you try
to speak,
you feel
their silence
overcoming you.

If you're silent,
you choke on *pain*
that they make you feel.
And if you speak,
you choke on *shame*
that they make you feel.

Sometimes we give love to the wrong person, and we wonder: *How could I have given love to that person? What a waste of time.* You shouldn't think about it this way. Instead, think of the fact that you were able to give love, because if you are able to give it, that means you have it within you. It is what makes you. And the same is true with kindness, honesty, and compassion. These things show who you are. Don't focus on the way people abuse your virtues. Focus on the fact that you have them. They make you a beautiful person, a beautiful human being. Before you think, *I wish I hadn't given love,* or, *I wish I hadn't been kind,* consider what those gifts say about you.

II

TURNING TO ASHES

Sometimes I feel
my soul so heavily,
as if it's a burden
on the air I breathe.

Pain comes when it comes,
not when you're ready for it.
And it leaves when it leaves,
not when you want it to.

When I tell you that
my pain falls asleep with me
and wakes up with me,
believe me.

Don't tell me I chose this pain.
No one chooses
this.

I was learning to throw pebbles,
and you gave me mountains
to carry.

I feel crippled every time
I think back
to how you silenced me.

I hate thinking of you
when you loved me.
It makes me
want to love you again.

What you tell your mind to avoid
is what your heart is truly seeking.

When we must let go of someone we love, we often wonder: *Why can't they love me? Is something wrong with me? Am I not good enough?* We start to equate our self-worth with how willing they are to love us, when the truth could be that it simply wasn't meant to be. The person who is meant for you, the person who is meant to give you the kind of love that you need, and, more importantly, the kind of love that you deserve, could be somewhere out there just waiting for you to notice them. Stop fixating on someone who gave you a feeling for a short period of time. You don't deserve to spend the rest of your life convincing someone of why they should love you.

Don't let your heart become numb. No matter how much pain you're going through, the solution should never be to become numb. The solution is to accept that any harm that was aimed at you is not your fault. And the pain that others choose to inflict on you is not because of who you are but because of who they are. If you become numb just to avoid the pain, then you won't be able to feel happiness either. Feel the pain, and resist the temptation to avoid it. If you can do that, you're a hero.

Stop setting yourself up for failure.
Don't give them a chance
to put you down.
Make the choice
to walk away,
and if you've already left,
decide that you'll never
go back.

Fall asleep with nothing
but love and forgiveness
in your heart.
What's meant for you
will be there for you
tomorrow or the day after.

Trust your journey.
Rest your soul.

I know that forgiveness is best,
but I hope that you never ask
for mine,
because
I don't believe
I am ready to forgive you.
I will feel like I have to
because
that is who I am.
My heart aches if I don't forgive
when I am asked,
and you've gotten used to asking.
You make mistakes
because
you know that I will forgive them.

Stop accepting less than what you deserve.
It does not make you a better person
unless you sacrifice for humanity—
not people who don't know
how or when
to stop taking.

When they don't like
that you speak the truth,
they will try
to change your reality.
They will create a world
where your truth
is considered insanity.

Does my name remind you
of me?
Or does it remind you
of the pain you caused me?
Do my words remind you
of why you loved me?
Or of the lies you made up about me?
Is that why you avoid me?
Is that why you block
every opportunity
to see me
or hear my name?

What a shame it is
for you to run away from
the truth of what you did to me
when I should be the one
running away from you.

You light the fire in front of me
and then you blame me for playing with it.
Don't tell me that you love me
and then blame me for falling in love
with you.

I want to complain to you
about you.

I want to cry to you
about you.
Perhaps the *you* who I loved
can tell the *you* who left
to come back home.

You say you want
a good woman,
and here I am
standing in front of you
with goodness pouring
out of my soul,
yet you see right through me
as if I don't exist.

You say you want
a faithful woman,
and here I am
with commitment beaming
out of my eyes,
yet you look right past me
as if you don't care
about honesty.

You say you want
a woman who loves you
for who you are,
and here I am with love
spilling from my heart
for you.
Yet you no longer look at me.
It's as though the beauty of my soul
has expired
and it's time for you to find
a new woman
while I sit here and wonder
what it is about me that
you once thought was magic
and you now see as a
dusty antique
that you no longer wish
to marvel at,
crave,
or touch.

Rejection hurts
even if it's from someone
you no longer want.
A knife in your heart
hurts no less
if you don't want it there.

I do not want you to apologize.
I do not want you to be sorry that
I felt that way.
I want you to be sorry for
what you did.
To feel sorry for
making me feel
the way that you did.

When home doesn't feel like home:
I drive around in circles
hoping to get to a destination—
one where I would be happy.
The right place.
The right time.
But it seems so impossible.

Where I leave from and
where I arrive
feel the same.

The ones who are supposed to
love you
don't love you.
So you run to those who
were never supposed to love you
but tend to love
people like you
who need love
so they can be loved in return.
Because those who were supposed to
love them
did not love them either.

It's been awhile
since I finally accepted
the end.
But my heart still aches
every time I think
of how we ended.
And if I could go back,
I wish I could tell you:
I stayed for so long,
not because I was weak
but because I believed
in the good person in you.
I left, not because
you stopped wanting me
but because I no longer
loved myself by loving you.

You are so hurt
but so kind.
You can't even tell them
"You hurt me."
You worry about
hurting their feelings
by telling them
that they hurt you.
How beautiful
is that kindness pouring
out of you?

I am so tired of
carrying this pain
that was never mine
in the first place.

Always give love.
Always be kind.
Always give your best.
If the world hurts
you
because of that,
know that
you
are creating a better world.

The world sees that
you are in pain
and says:
Let me give you a little more.
You've handled this much.
You can handle a bit more.

I don't have to look like
I'm in pain
for me to be
in pain.

Your friends will say:
"I miss you."
You'll say:
"I miss me too."

I was telling them
that I was in pain
without telling them.
I was hoping they would see
my wings turn into ashes.
I was hoping
they would wonder why the fire
that was once in my eyes
was now burning
the life
out of me.

They want to know
why you're feeling sad,
but when you finally speak,
they make you wish
that you never spoke.

I come to the coffee shop
when I have no one to meet,
and I sip on my coffee
slowly.
I look out the window
waiting for no one to come,
slowly.

I can't remember when
I stopped waiting for
someone.
And I can't remember when
I started finding love
in my pen and paper,
in the lipstick stain on
the rim of my coffee cup.

I can't remember when
I started finding love in myself
and stopped waiting to find it
in someone else.

You're not the only one
who's not happy.
Trust me.
All you see is what you want
but don't have.

People like you are hiding
behind smiles,
pretending to be happy
while they're wondering
why they don't have what
others have,
just like you are.

Some hearts ache from holding
too much hatred.
Mine aches from holding
too much love.

You may not see them suffer
like they made you suffer.
But believe me,
their biggest punishment
is that they are who they are.

Your heart might be in pain right now,
but it will heal.
It will heal.
You will heal.

I don't even know
what I want anymore.
I want love,
but not just anyone's love.
And men fall for me
like dead leaves in autumn.
I want them to fall
for me,
but I don't want to catch them.
I don't want
them.
Is it fear?
Or is it me wanting to know
what it feels like to have someone
fall off a cliff
flat on their face
as I once did for someone
who enjoyed watching me fall
only to walk away
the moment I hit the ground?
The moment that my soul shattered
and I was no longer
the person
I used to be?

A man I barely knew
looked at the tears
that built a home in my eyes
and said:
"Your soul is too beautiful
for you to cry."
That's when my tears
escaped my eyes
and I said:
"How will my soul be pure
if I don't cleanse
the pain with my tears?"

I just want to breathe,
and I am gasping for air,
but my lungs feel too small.
I guess that is what happens when
your lungs enter
survival mode—
they breathe only as much
as they need
to stay alive.

This air that wants to
enter you
and this love that wants to enter you
have no room to stay inside of you.
That's why it's so hard
for you to accept
new love.
It's too much to handle.

Your insides have been
the home of abuse
for so long
that love hurts
as it enters.

The parts of me
that want to care
are too hurt
to even pretend to care.

I feel that I am on the verge
of disappearing,
of surrendering into nothingness,
of accepting that I am worth
absolutely nothing
and that I deserve what happened to me.
And everything that it did to me.
I have no power.
Where do I get it from?

I am broken
beyond repair.

There is no going back
to the person I was before.

There is rebirth,
rebuilding,
reinventing,
and soul stitching
with gold
that needs to happen.

Your sensitivity is not a sign of weakness. Your sensitivity makes you beautiful. It makes you unique. You see, we live in a world where it's easier to pretend that you don't feel, and if you dare express that you feel, you become an easy target to be picked on and hurt. So, from a young age, you're taught that strength means hiding how you feel, or not expressing your feelings at all. I want you to ask yourself, if you don't feel, how can you truly love? If you don't feel, how can you empathize with the tragedies happening in the world? If you are sensitive to being disrespected, it means that you will not disrespect others because you know how it feels to be disrespected. If you are sensitive to being ignored or lied to, you will not ignore or lie to others because you know how it feels to be ignored and lied to. Promise yourself from today to be at peace with your sensitivity. Instead of trying to hide it, cherish it.

III

SPARKS OF PHOENIX

The one who broke you
cannot heal you.

Sometimes
we, the fixers,
need fixing too.
Sometimes
we, the givers,
need gifts too.

Your heart broke
in pieces.
It will heal
in pieces
too.

A voice from within me
roars
and lifts me
from the rubble
that I've become.
It lifts me from this darkness
I've been in for far too long.
It reminds me that my eyes
have adapted to the dark
but there is so much more for me to see.

Even when it feels like the end,
it's not the end.

You are bigger than
what's pulling you down.
Shake the ashes
off your wings and
rise.
Fly.
Soar.

When they make the mistake
and you have to apologize,
know that there is a problem
and walk away.

What turns into
hatred
was never
love.

The world took care of me when
I believed that I didn't deserve
to be cared for.

An end
does not have to be
the end.

Give your heart time to heal.
The poison of pain took time to enter.
It will take time to leave.

It's okay for you
to be angry about
what happened to you.
Just don't let your anger
make you like the one
who broke you.
Stay true to yourself.

Just as you need to
own your pain,
you need to
own your healing.

Just because they took advantage
of your kindness,
you do not
blame your kindness
for the pain.

Your kindness
is not weakness.
Their taking advantage
of your kindness
is weakness.

It's easier for them to believe
that something is wrong with you
than it is for them to believe
that something wrong happened to you.

You are only a threat to
those who don't believe in
their
own worth.

You are bigger than
the place that did not welcome you.
The person who rejected you.
The humans who did not value you.
You are bigger.

Don't lose yourself
looking for love inside
of someone else.
If you lose yourself,
no one else's love will
make you feel whole or
found or
home.

My home will never welcome me
if I don't welcome myself.

Your biggest loss was me.
My biggest loss was me.

There is no going back
to the moments when you fell in love
with me.

You can never
unscar me.
The damage is done.
I must love my new self.

My scars are witnesses
that I never gave up.

You fell out of love
with me
so the world
could fall in love with me.

What they did to you will never
be okay.
But you will be.

Forgiving them frees you,
not them.

You will stay
in ashes
if you base your rising
on their apology.

If I am not worth your apology,
you are not worth me carrying
the pain that you caused me.
So I will forgive you, not for you
but for me.
I deserve to let go.
I deserve to be free of your pain.
And if you
can't admit your own mistakes,
I will not allow the ashes that your pain
turned me into
to hold me hostage.

Don't forgive them because
you *have* to
but because you *want* to.
And don't forgive them when
you *have* to
but when *you are ready.*

You can't erase
what happened to you,
but you can choose
to put it behind you,
under your feet,
and rise like
the hero you are.

You owe it to the glory within you
to become so much more
than who
they
want
you
to be.

The reason is coming.
Don't wait.
You'll slow down
its arrival
if you do.

There is a heart inside of you
waiting to be loved by you.
Don't let it down.
Don't let yourself down.

You will never heal from a pain
that you don't admit you have.
You will never heal from a pain
that you don't
allow yourself to feel.

Give yourself approval before
you expect it from someone
else.

I sat down with my words.
I wanted to write about you
just once more.

My words revolted.
They refused to help.
They abandoned me,
just as you did.

And just as I chased after
what I thought was left of
us,
I chased after them.

My words told me
that they no longer wanted
to be about you.
They said
it was a disgrace for them
to be written
and rewritten
once more
about someone like you.

The pages are too full
and the lines have
no more room
for the same old story.

I must turn the page.
and start anew.

I must start
a new story
about someone new.

Your heart won't heal
as long as it stays
in the same place where
pain entered it.

There is fear in the unknown.
But fear
does not mean
settling.
It does not mean stopping.
Your fears are not meant
to keep you in fear.
They are meant
to keep you moving.

Your fears are meant
to make you rise.

Let them judge you.
They will live with their
judgment,
and you will live
with your truth.

It was not those I loved
who hurt me the most
but those I trusted.

There is a difference.

You are not defined by
who respects you but
by who you respect.

You are not
the pain that broke you.
You are who it made you become.

They will curse the day
that they chose to deny
your story.

If they are talking about you behind your back, shame on them. Let them talk. If someone spends their time talking about you negatively, what does that say about them?

If they blame you for what you went through, let them blame you. You know what happened to you. If they blame you for burning in a fire someone put you through, that speaks of them, not of you. Instead of helping you heal, they are telling you that your soul's burning was your own fault. You don't need people like that in your life.

If they see you screaming for help and pretend not to hear, let them turn away. Their refusal to act does not mean that you don't have a voice. It means that they are in denial of the effort they need to make to cause change.

Those who don't have the courage to acknowledge that you've been wronged are complicit in your harm. They are bystanders. Don't take that lightly. Anyone who stays quiet during your time of need either does not care about you, is too afraid to show you their support, or doesn't believe you. And you don't need to think of any of those people during your time of struggle. Continue to care about them if you do; show them support when they need it; and believe them when they speak their truth. Because that is who *you* are. But don't let their lack of support make you feel unworthy. Their stances show their character, not yours.

Last but not least, remember that staying true to yourself is the most important thing. Don't allow gossip, hypocrisy, misogyny, or bias to bring you down. You are way ahead of those things. And you are standing by the truth by standing up against them. Whoever you are and wherever you are—keep going. Keep fighting. Keep being a warrior. Do not give up.

IV

THE RISING

From the ashes,
I rose
and I stitched the pieces
of my soul
back together
with gold.

My wings are no longer broken.
My wings are hurting,
but they are healing.

There are days when
pain wakes up with you.
Welcome it.

Strength does not mean
that you have no struggle
or that you are completely
at peace
with a hurtful past.
It means that you
don't allow the past
to make you
shrink
and fall again.

If they can't love
the broken pieces of you,
they won't be able to love
the whole you.

Your pieces make you—
broken or back together.

I sometimes feel that
I can't live with myself
because of what you did
to me
and got away with.
Then I remember:
How could you
live with yourself
knowing what you did
to me?
I will not live with your guilt.
I will not carry your weight.
It is yours to carry.

You hit me with
your pain
and I turn it into
poetry.

You look at me and wonder
how I can be so strong while
I am fighting wars inside.
Some days I win.
Some days I lose.
But both days, I smile.

How dare you tell me
that I am only hurt
because you no longer want me.
You don't put a knife
in someone's heart and twist
and twist
and twist
then tell them that
that they're only hurt
because you are no longer
twisting.

No one has the right to judge the pain inside of your heart. They are not the ones who sit by your bedside when you cry yourself to sleep at night. They are not the ones who carry the mountains on your shoulders as you get through the day. They are not the ones who are wondering where your happiness went. They are not the ones aching to smile again. No one should ever judge a pain they've never felt. Those who love you don't judge you. They listen to you. They understand you. And they love the pain out of you. They don't try to beat the pain out of you by denying you the right to feel it. So don't feel ashamed that you're in pain just because someone makes you feel that you have no right to feel it.

Don't say
"I don't have a choice."
Don't say
"I don't have a voice."
Stand up for yourself.

I will be anything but
silenced.

If the voice inside your head
is not yours,
shut it up and
kick it out.

The past is behind you
for a reason.
Don't go back to it
hoping that it will change.
No one can change history.
It already happened.
No one can make a day that ended
start again.
If you try to change the past,
it will only break you again.

You cannot change
a beginning
that began in the past.
You can end it
and start a new beginning
that begins now.

If you speak and
they don't like what you have to say,
they will try to silence you.

Don't lose hope.
Your pain will be
seen
and felt.
Your voice will be
heard
and echoed.

The world has so much goodness
in its heart for you.
And it will
fall into you.
Be patient.

We don't relive our pain
because we want to
but because it took
parts of us
that we can never get back.

We are grieving while
healing.

I told you once:
"I'd hate to write a heartbreak poem
about you one day."
You got angry and said:
"That would never happen.
I already promised you
that I will never walk away."
But here I am,
writing pages and chapters
to cleanse my soul of the pain
that you promised to protect me from.

Just because your love for me
was not real,
I will not deny my love for you.
I am proud to have a heart
that loves sincerely
and a soul that smiled innocently
for every poem you wrote me.

Even though your words
turned out to be
just words,
I thank you
for allowing me to feel
how much love my heart could give.
I thank you
for showing me
that my heart could survive
one more break.
Thank you.

It's okay to never be okay
with what happened to you.
Just remember that
not being okay with it
does not mean that you
can't move
past it.
It might never stop never being okay,
but you will be okay.

You tried to silence me
by putting my own hands over
my mouth.
My hands melted into my face,
and all of my words transformed
into action.
Thank you.

Don't blame *yourself*
for *their*
unwillingness
to put in the effort
to fix *their* mistakes.

I know you're tired,
but you have to keep going.
Remember *where* you want to be.
Remember *who* you want to be.
Don't allow yourself to give up.
It may be an option,
but don't you choose it.
You deserve more.

Don't lose hope.
The truth always wins.

You have every right to feel your pain.
You have every right to feel unheard
when they don't listen.
You have every right to bleed,
to grieve,
every time they stab you.
Do not allow their belittling of
your pain
to make you
ashamed
of how you feel.

Don't live your life in fear
of what they said
or what they'll say
or what they might say.
Live your truth,
and be true to yourself.

They will never be able to
feel
how much they hurt you
even if you scream it
into their hearts.
If they were able to feel as you do,
they would not have hurt you,
so
stop crumbling in front of them.
They will not pick up the pieces of
you.
You have to do that.

The first time I saw you in a coffee shop
after you denied the whole story
of us,
you got up and left
the moment you saw me.
That hurt so much.
And you will never know because
I will never tell you.
It reminded me of you
letting go.
It reminded me of you
walking away.
I cried, not because I missed you
but because I hate that I had to see you.
I hate you.
I hate you.
I hate you.
That is what I really want to say.
I've tried so hard not to,
but
I have to.
I hate you.

How did it feel
to have someone like me
love you?
Did my innocence remind you
of what you had before
you turned into the devil
that you are now?
Did the spark in my eyes
give you a fire
to put out?
Did the softness of my skin
soothe the thorns on yours?
Did the warmth of my heart
melt the coldness of yours?
Well,
here is the strength of my vulnerability
exposing the weakness of your manipulation.

Excuse me, sir.
I see you looking in the wrong place.
You look at my face
as if there is nothing to see
other than
the color of my eyes,
the fairness of my skin,
or the adventures that my body might take you on.
You look at my body
as if there is nothing to see
other than
the curves of mountains and valleys,
as if my body is a land for you
to journey,
to discover,
to occupy.
Excuse me, sir.
My body is not a place for your conquest.
Don't get me wrong—
I am a mystery.
I am a masterpiece.
I carry with my body
the cities of the world.
I have, carved, on my body
streets that you want me to hide
because you see them as scars.
I have, built, in my eyes,
blazing fires that you want to put out
because you are afraid
to get burned.
And if you dare to venture, sir,
beyond the color of my eyes,
beyond the touch of my skin,
beyond the places on my body
that you want to own,

you will find oceans
that you will drown in
if you are not ready to sail.
You will find mountains of wisdom
that I have inherited from every woman, every mother, every girl
on this earth.
If you dare to venture beyond my skin,
you will find skies filled with love and compassion that
centuries of women have instilled within me.
The problem, sir,
is that you want to own parts of me
instead of honor the depths of me.
But what you should know, sir,
is that only
I
own
the map.

I am not a land for you to occupy.
I am not a ship for you to steer.
I am not a fire for you to contain.
I am not a property for you to put a price on.

Whether I am young, old, or in-between,
who I am and what I give to this world
is not defined by the canvas that your eyes
paint my body on.
You see, sir, the way that you see me
says a lot more about you
than it says about me.
The way that you devalue
the treasures in me
says a lot more about you
than it says about me.

The way that you define the beauty of me
with the pleasure that you get
out of me
says a lot more about you
than it says about me.
I am beautiful,
not because of my face,
not because of my body.
I am beautiful because of the heart
contained in this body.
I am beautiful because of the mind
controlling this body.
So if you must *grab* me by something,
let it be my heart.
It is what makes the world
a compassionate place.
If you must *grab* me by something,
let it be my mind.
It is what spreads wisdom in this world
like wildfire.
And finally, sir,
I must ask you:
If the woman in me
sees the human in you,
why can't the man in you
see the human in me?

For all the times
you saw me and
pretended not to see me or
didn't want to be seen with me:

A day will come
when I will no longer
want to be seen by you or
seen around you.
It will be you
waving at me
from across the street
and it will be me
turning in the other direction.

I want you to leave
my place of peace
as you've left me in
your place of turmoil.

When you are tempted
to wish them pain,
remember how it felt
when they hurt you.

Never wish them pain.
That's not who you are.
If they caused you pain,
they must have pain inside.
Wish them healing.
That's what they need.

It's sad how
you disappoint those
who let you down
when you speak of how
they let you down.

I stopped longing
to be understood
when the ones I thought
understood me
in my darkness
turned out to have knives
hidden under their tongues.

To all of the lights
who chose to dim
when I was in the darkness,
thank you for teaching me
that my own light
is all I need.

It feels like I have to
believe myself
and
teach people how to
believe me.

It feels like I have to
heal myself
and
teach people how to
help me heal.

Don't tell me how
or when
to heal
if you didn't live through my pain,
if your heart did not stop
and struggle
to be with mine
when I was burning
and turning to ashes.

Lose as many people as you need to
in order to not lose yourself.
No one worth keeping
in your life
is worth you
losing yourself.

When a hero is rising,
many will choose
to focus on the ashes at their feet.
Keep rising.
You are about
to start soaring.

V

THE SOARING

I am so proud
of the warrior
I've created
from the ashes
that were meant
to bury me.

You are a soaring reminder of what they
cannot
have.

Look down
at your pain
all the way from the sky.
Look how small it is.

Look at how big
the world is.
Look at all of the streets
you can take.
Look at all of the mountains
you can climb
and soar above.

I have poems
and books
inside of me
waiting to be written
from the pain of humans
whose names history
will not remember
or miss.

When his voice
asks me now:
Who do you think you are?
the hero I've become
answers:
I am Najwa Zebian.
I am a hero.
I am a survivor.

A woman asks me:
"How could a man
like him
not want
a woman like you?"
The younger, more innocent me would say:
"Try sitting in my seat.
Try to understand
this
while being me."
The older, wiser me says:
"He wants me,
but not in the way that
I want to be wanted.
He wants my untouched body
to be his heaven for one night
so he can leave it empty,
like his hollow soul."
*Don't mistake his
lust for love.*

I know that my kindness
hurts me,
but I will continue to choose it,
not because I'm naive
but because *my* actions define *me.*

Remind your heart that kindness
is always the answer.

If your pain doesn't make
your soul softer and kinder
with everyone around you,
then you are not using your pain
in the right way.
You can be angry
that you're in pain.
You can be upset
that you don't deserve
to be in pain.
Or you can be humble enough to say:

Pain is part of life.
And my ability to feel it
proves that I am human.

My wounds teach me
not to hurt others.

My scars have become
my friends.
They remind me
of how brave I was
to overcome
the pain of my wounds.

There is a part of me
that craves
not needing safety.
I no longer want safety.
I am a free bird
soaring.

To be kind
in a world that could be
so cruel
to kind souls
like you
must be the greatest
act of courage.

I heard
you're hurting
because of what I said about you.
I heard you're hurting
because of how I made
you look in the eyes of others.
I think you're hurting
because you know that you
made a mistake
by hurting me.
I think you're hurting
because of who I became,
because of who I am becoming.
And because you no longer
have the honor of being the one I love.

You are no longer someone I love.
You are someone I once loved.

Why should I feel bad
for you?
Why should I feel guilty
for not wondering
how you are dealing
with your truth being exposed?

When you were torturing me,
did you
for one moment
wonder how I was dealing
with what you
were putting me through?

I will never be okay
with what you did to me.
You have to be okay with that.

Regret without an apology is
cowardice.

It was not you
who I loved.
It was the person
I thought you were.
It was the person
you made me believe you were.
Not you.

I am free,
not because
you let me go.
I am free because
I let you go.
And set myself free.

I will not thank you for this pain.
I will not thank you for this destruction.
But I thank you for this lesson:

My demolition might not be in my hands,
but my reconstruction is.

Now that I have built my own home,
in every place
or person that I try to make my home,
my soul feels rejected.
My own home
feels like I am abandoning it.

The most painful rejection
is rejection of the self.
The soul's denial of itself.
The heart's refusal to love
itself before it's loved
by someone else.

If you hate me because of
what happened to me,
I don't hate you,
but
I also will not allow your hatred
of me to make me doubt myself.

I don't want to be liked
by someone whose love is
conditional on shame.

If I lost your respect because
of what I went through,
keep your respect.
I don't want it.

You don't have to be okay
with me
or with what I did with
what happened to me
for me to be okay
with myself.

It will be a glorious moment
when you realize
that it is the world,
not humans,
that will give to you
from its heart
based on your intentions.

You can be a fighter
and have pain inside of you.
You can be a hero
and live with trauma.
You can be brave
and still need a break.

Give love from your soul
because you want to.
Because it feels right.
Not because you have to.
Take love
because you want to,
not because you're afraid
of saying no.
Not because you're afraid
of being alone.

Look how far you've come.
You rose above
what was meant to break you.
You are soaring.
You are a hero
reborn.

VI

A NEW CHAPTER

I have been soaring
for a while now,
and I am afraid
of burning again.

He said to me:
"I know you're broken.
I know your soul has been shattered.
But you are beautiful
in a way that I cannot explain.
And I think that
being in love with you
would be
the beginning and end
of all beauty."

He told me:
"Smile for once."
Silly boy, my heart's been smiling
since the moment you said:
"You can trust me."
Since the moment you took my pen
and wrote
"Trust me"
on the pages of the journal
of my heart.

I'm afraid to allow love in
again
because I don't know
what love is anymore.
For a while now,
love has been pain.
I want to shield myself from pain
again,
so I tell you
that I don't want you to love me
because
you feel bad for me.

You tell me that
you can force people to do anything
except love.
You cannot force people to love you.
He says:
"You cannot,
did not,
and will not
force me to love you.
I just do.
I choose to love you.
And there is nothing
you can do to force yourself
out of my heart."

Why do you want to love me?
I will traumatize you.

I hear your words
through my wounds.
I see your face
through my wounds.
I talk to you
through my wounds.
And I will love you
through my wounds,
just like your love will enter me
through my wounds.

"Look at me."
Three words that cause
an earthquake in my bones.

I want to tell you
that I am falling for you,
but fear of this moment
stops me.
My heart reminds me:
Don't allow room
for shame.
Tell the people you love
that you love them.

He tells me:
"I wanted to get you
one rose,
but I thought about you
twelve times today,
so twelve roses
are what I got for
the sun standing in front of me."

My heart says:
One rose is enough.

He reminds me:
"Not for you."

I've never wanted roses
to resist wilting
more than I do now.
That's how I know
that I want this love
to last.

I tell you
there are things about me
you should know.
I'm afraid
they'll make you leave,
but I tell myself
that I will not hide
parts of who I am
because of the person
that I want you to see.

He tells me:

"Your history is written
in your eyes.
In the way that you
look down
and to the side,
anywhere but into my eyes."

He tells me:

"There is a truth that's hidden
in your eyes.
You're falling in love
or trying not to fall again.

And if you think
I don't know
what you've been through,
you must think
I'm foolish at
love."

I knew that our souls
were connected
when you told me:
"The sight of you
and the sound of your voice
stimulate my brain
more than
the touch of
all the women whose bodies
I have explored."

How do I tell you
not to compare me
to other women?
Not to love me more
because you love them less?
Because you love *her* less?

Love *me*
for who *I* am,
not who I'm *not*.
Love me because
you love
me.

You stayed a short while,
but
you made me want to write
about love,
not heartbreak,
again.
Thank you.

AN INVITATION

If this book has moved you, then move. Lift up your pen and start writing your own story, however you'd like to write it. Don't keep it inside of you if it needs to leave you. Don't settle in the ashes of your pain. Let the sparks lift you up. Rise from the ashes as I rose. And soar.

ACKNOWLEDGMENTS

Thank you
to every person who
loved me as I was burning
and turning to ashes,
not just as I was rising
and soaring.

Thank you
for loving me
when it was difficult.

ABOUT THE AUTHOR

Najwa Zebian is a Lebanese-Canadian author, speaker, and educator. Her passion for language was evident from a young age, as she delved into Arabic poetry and novels. The search for a home—what Najwa describes as a place where the soul and heart feel at peace—was central to her early years. When she arrived in Canada at the age of sixteen, she felt unstable and adrift in an unfamiliar place. Nevertheless, she completed her education and went on to become a teacher as well as a doctoral candidate in educational leadership. Her first students, a group of young refugees, led her back to her original passion: writing. She began to heal her sixteen-year-old self by writing to heal her students.

Since self-publishing her first collection of poetry and prose in 2016, Najwa has become an inspiration to millions of people worldwide. Drawing on her own experiences of displacement, discrimination, and abuse, Najwa uses her words to encourage others to build a home within themselves; to live, love, and create fearlessly.

Andrews McMeel Publishing
a division of Andrews McMeel Universal
1130 Walnut Street, Kansas City, Missouri 64106

www.andrewsmcmeel.com

19 20 21 22 23 BVG 10 9 8 7 6 5 4 3 2 1

ISBN: 978-1-4494-9620-3

Library of Congress Control Number: 2018945556

Editor: Melissa Rhodes
Art Director: Holly Swayne
Production Editor: Elizabeth A. Garcia
Production Manager: Cliff Koehler

ATTENTION: SCHOOLS AND BUSINESSES
Andrews McMeel books are available at quantity discounts with bulk purchase for educational, business, or sales promotional use. For information, please e-mail the Andrews McMeel Publishing Special Sales Department: specialsales@amuniversal.com.